FOOD SECURITY IN AFRICA'S SECONDARY CITIES: NO. 2. THE OSHAKATI-ONGWEDIVA-ONDANGWA CORRIDOR, NAMIBIA

NDEYAPO NICKANOR, LAWRENCE KAZEMBE
AND JONATHAN CRUSH

SERIES EDITOR: PROF. JONATHAN CRUSH

URBAN FOOD SECURITY SERIES NO. 28

ACKNOWLEDGEMENTS

This is the second publication in a new AFSUN series on the relationship between rapid urbanization, secondary cities, and food security in Africa. This case study is funded by an Insight Grant from the Social Sciences and Humanities Research Council of Canada (SSHRC) on *Secondary Urbanization, Food Security and Local Governance in Africa*.

Published by the African Food Security Urban Network (AFSUN)
www.afsun.org

First published 2019

ISBN 978-1-920597-39-9

Cover photo: Jonathan Crush

Production by Bronwen Dachs Muller, Cape Town

Printed by Print on Demand, Cape Town

AUTHORS

Ndeyapo Nickanor is Dean in the Faculty of Science at the University of Namibia, Windhoek.

Lawrence Kazembe is Associate Professor in the Department of Statistics and Population Studies, Faculty of Science, University of Namibia, Windhoek.

Jonathan Crush is Professor at the Balsillie School of International Affairs, and University Research Professor, Wilfrid Laurier University, Waterloo, Canada.

Previous Publications in the AFSUN Series

CONTENTS

TABLES

FIGURES

1. INTRODUCTION

Since 2008, the African Food Security Urban Network (AFSUN) has focused its attention on major cities in Southern Africa, documenting the high levels of food insecurity and urban poverty, poor dietary diversity, and the daunting challenges of incorporating food security concerns into policy and governance (Crush and Battersby, 2016; Frayne et al., 2018). Much of AFSUN's urban food security research in Namibia to date has focused on the capital city of Windhoek (Pendleton et al., 2012, Nickanor et al., 2016). This is not surprising as Windhoek is the country's largest city, containing over one-third of the urbanized population, and is a major convergence point for social and economic development as well as rural-to-urban migration. AFSUN's 2008 Windhoek household food security survey found that more than 76% of households in the city's informal settlements were severely food insecure (Pendleton et al., 2012; Nickanor et al., 2016). By 2016, the severely food insecure in the city's informal settlements had increased to more than 90% (Nickanor et al., 2017). These extremely high levels suggest a deteriorating food security situation amid continued rapid urbanization.

In the 1990s, urbanization in the north attracted considerable attention from researchers at the University of Namibia. Studies of Oshakati showed not only the severe poverty and inequality in the town, but also provided insights into its demographic composition (Tvedten and Hangula, 1994; Tvedten and Pomuti, 1994; Tvedten and Nangula, 1999; Tvedten, 2006). However, none of these studies focused explicitly on food insecurity. Further, much has changed since the early 1990s, not only the size of Oshakati, but also its connectivity with Ongwediva and Ondangwa, with Windhoek, and with southern Angola after the civil war there ended in 2002. As well as providing contemporary insights into the demographic and economic make-up of Oshakati and the other towns, this report suggests that the urban food system is a powerful lens for viewing urban challenges by linking the daily experiences of food provisioning with social and economic relationships, poverty and inequality, ecological sustainability, and the global political economy (Crush, 2014). Food in urban areas has conventionally been subordinated to problems such as housing, sanitation, road infrastructure, and security. However, food is central to urban life and therefore provides a way of understanding urban vulnerabilities.

The central question this report sets out to answer is whether the poverty and food security situation in Namibia's smaller urban centres is any better than in the capital. The report also provides the opportunity to make systematic comparisons between Windhoek and secondary urban centres in Namibia across a range of variables. The household survey on which the report is based is part of AFSUN's current focus on raising the profile of food systems, food security, and food governance in secondary cities in Africa. The project links the Balsillie School of International Affairs in Canada with partners in Namibia (University of Namibia), Malawi (University of Livingstonia) and Cameroon (University of Dschang). In Namibia, the project's focus is on the three northern towns of Oshakati, Ongwediva, and Ondangwa. The Oshakati-Ongwediva-Ondangwa urban corridor case study research is led by the University of Namibia with funding from the Social Sciences and Humanities Research Council of Canada.

2. Secondary Urbanization in Namibia

2.1 Namibia's Urban Hierarchy

At independence in 1990, the total urban population of Namibia was estimated at 28%. It had grown to 33% by 2001 and to 42% by 2011. UNHABITAT (2016) estimates that the current level of urbanization is 47% and that this will grow to 55% by 2025. Namibia is an excellent example of urban primacy with Windhoek easily the largest city in the country's urban hierarchy. In 2011, Windhoek's population of 322,500 constituted 37% of the total urban population of the country (Table 1). The second largest centre was Rundu in the northeast on the border with Angola at 63,400, making it only one-fifth of the size of Windhoek.

At the same time, the country has a considerable number of smaller urban centres with 10 towns with populations of between 25,000 and 65,000 in 2011. Most of these towns have experienced continuous, and in some cases particularly rapid, growth since the 1980s. Several of these fast-growing secondary urban centres are in the north. Rundu, for example, grew from fewer than 1,000 people in 1981 to over 60,000 in 2011 and increased its ranking in the urban hierarchy from 24th to second. Another fast-growing town is Katima Mulilo, from a population of 575 in 1981 to 28,200 in 2011. Some of the fastest-growing secondary centres, and the subject of this report, are Oshakati, Ongwediva, and Ondangwa located in north-central Namibia.

TABLE 1: Urbanization in Namibia, 1981-2011				
	1981	1991	2001	2011
Windhoek	96,057	147,056	233,529	325,858
Rehoboth	12,378	21,439	21,308	29,232
Swakopmund	12,219	17,681	23,808	44,725
Keetmanshoop	11,502	15,032	15,778	19,447
Tsumeb	11,296	14,929	16,211	19,275
Otjiwarongo	9,087	15,921	19,614	28,163
Grootfontein	7,536	12,829	14,249	16,632
Okahandla	6,721	11,040	14,039	22,639
Gobabis	5,528	8,340	13,856	19,101
Mariental	5,367	7,581	9,836	12,478
Khorixas	5,349	7,358	5,890	6,796
Luderitz	4,748	7,700	13,295	12,537
Opuwo	4,186	4,234	5,101	7,657
Oranjemund	4,112	7,801	4,451	3,908
Okakarara	3,941	3,725	3,296	4,709
Oshakati	3,684	21,603	28,255	36,541
Karasburg	3,484	4,602	4,075	4,401
Omaruru	2,982	4,851	4,761	6,300
Usakos	2,852	3,548	2,926	3,585
Outjo	2,504	4,535	6,103	8,445
Otavi	2,137	3,506	3,813	5,245
Karibib	1,608	3,067	3,726	5,132
Ondangwa	1,000	7,926	10,900	22,822
Rundu	989	19,366	44,413	63,431
Katima Mulilo	575	13,377	22,694	28,362
Walvis Bay	–	22,999	43,611	62,096
Ongwediva	–	6,197	10,742	20,260
Source: Regional Profiles. Namibia Statistics Agency, 2014				

2.2 History of Urbanization in Northern Namibia

Oshakati and Ondangwa were the first northern colonial towns in Owamboland (as it came to be called). Owamboland has about eight ethnic groups with similarities in language, culture, farming and land cultivation practices. Following the first world war and the transfer of the colony from German to South African control, South Africa intensified the policy of land expropriation for white settlers. After the second world war, illiterate, poor white Afrikaners were given expropriated land and support from government in the form of cash loans (without need for repayment), farm supplies, boreholes for water, cattle, seeds, and schools.

The 1962 Odendaal Commission argued that the development of the country could only be achieved by the white population and provided for the division of Namibia into 11 districts along ethnic and racial lines (RSA, 1962). Indigenous Namibians were driven into reserves where resources were scarce and subsistence was meagre. Owamboland was one of these reserves (Botha, 2005; Melber, 2005). In total, the reserves constituted about 40% of the total land area of the country, 43% was held as private property by whites, and the remainder was under government control as natural reserves or mining areas. Apartheid practices intensified and by the 1970s much of the productive farmland in Namibia was occupied by white farmers. As indigenous people lost their livelihoods, freedoms, and land, they also lost control over natural resources.

Under German and South African colonial rule, coercive measures were used to force indigenous people to work on the mines and commercial farms of Namibia (then called South West Africa). The northern districts of Owamboland, Kavango, and Caprivi were effectively segregated and controlled as a "police zone" (Werner, 1993). These areas experienced little development and emigration was restricted to men who had labour contracts that required them to return when the contract was over (Moorsom, 1977). A contract labour recruiting organization, SWANLA, was established in 1943. Operated from Ondangwa, it provided contract labourers mainly from Owamboland (Werner, 1993). In 1972, an estimated 50% of men from Owamboland were away working on contracts in towns, farms, and mines.

A veterinary cordon fence had been set up in 1896 to separate the northern communal areas and to control the movement of people and goods from these areas. Within the "police zones" of Namibia, small towns were established to service the settler economy, while most business, transportation, and government functions were centralized in Windhoek. Movement of the indigenous population to and within these towns was controlled by a system of permits, which were required for travel within towns, and from the communal reserves and farms (Pendleton and Frayne, 1998). Other repressive laws governed marriage, employment, and basic civil rights.

The three towns of Oshakati, Ondangwa, and Ongwediva were established at different times and for different reasons. Ondangwa, a royal seat, is the oldest town in north-central Namibia and the first Christian mission in Owamboland was established there as early as 1870. In 1966, South Africa established Oshakati as the administrative capital of Owamboland. During the 1980s, South Africa used Oshakati as a base for its economic intervention in northern Namibia as well as for its military operations against the liberation movement during the Namibian War of Independence (Hangula, 1993; Dale, 2014). Large military structures were established, as well as hospitals, schools, a meat-processing plant, and several small factories. Both Oshakati and Ondangwa grew rapidly during the 1970s and 1980s because of the presence of the South African army of occupation, as well as in-migration from the countryside and the arrival of refugees from the Angolan civil war. In 1981, only 3,684 people lived in Oshakati and this number had grown to 22,000 by 1991. Ongwediva was only founded in the early 1990s after independence.

After 1990, Oshakati became an important trading hub for the region, and by 2011 its population had increased to 35,600. Ondangwa grew in similar fashion but at a slower pace. Between 2001 and 2011, however, its population almost doubled to 21,100. Ongwediva grew quickly and had a population of nearly 20,000 by 2011. These three towns have been major centres of post-independence development in the north and are in close proximity to one another. Oshakati and Ongwediva are 5km apart and Ondangwa is 30km from Ongwediva. They constitute an urban corridor with a combined population of over 100,000 and share an airport located in Ondangwa. They are also the hub of trans-border trade with Angola.

Owamboland has been split into four regions (Omusati, Oshana, Oshikoto, and Ohangwena) with a combined population of nearly one million people. Oshakati, Ongwediva, and Ondangwa are in the Oshana region and serve this densely populated area of the country. Until recently, Ongwediva was primarily a high-income residential area with a workforce of nurses, teachers, and other professionals who commuted to work in Oshakati. Ongwediva now has many of its own facilities, which complement those in Oshakati; for example, the major public hospital is in Oshakati, but Ongwediva has a private hospital (where a historic kidney transplant took place in 2017). The engineering campus of the University of Namibia is located in Ongwediva, while Oshakati hosts part of the university's nursing science school. Ondangwa is the site of the engineering campus's industrial park.

FIGURE 1: Location of Oshakati-Ongwediva-Ondangwa Urban Corridor

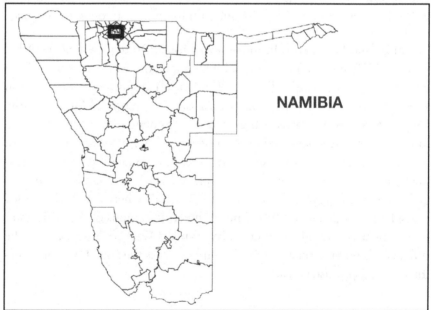

2.3 Urban Geography of Oshakati-Ongwediva-Ondangwa

All three towns are surrounded by *oshanas* (inland water channels), palm trees, communal farmland, and settlements. An important physical characteristic of Oshakati is that an estimated 50% of the urban area is covered by *oshanas*, which are prone to flooding (Tshilunga, 2014). In terms of the urban geography of the corridor, the apartheid regime divided Oshakati along racial lines into Oshakati East (for whites) and Oshakati West (for blacks). All of apartheid South Africa's regulations of separate development and restricted movement were implemented in draconian fashion. However, Oshakati West was unable to accommodate the growing population and various informal settlements were established including Oshoopala, Evululuku, Uupindi, and Oneshila (Figure 2).

At independence in 1990, around 85% of the population lived in informal settlements (Tvedten, 2006: 40). Town planning for Oshakati and Ondangwa has been haphazard, with a collection of residential complexes, major shopping complexes (with banking services), and *cuca* shops (bars) along the main road. Taxis, donkey carts, and luxury vehicles compete for space on the road. Proximity to the communal areas has meant that there are strong rural-urban linkages, which is a feature of secondary urban centres in Africa more generally. These towns serve as the first point of contact with urbanism of the rural population, with many people moving on to other urban areas, especially Windhoek.

FIGURE 2: Residential Geography of Oshakati

Source: Ministry of Lands and Resettlement

Figure 3 shows the growth in informal settlements in Oshakati since 1991. The 2011 Census recorded 2,113 shacks in the town. However, as Weber and Mendelsohn (2017) point out, Oshakati's informal settlements also contain many brick/block houses. In total, 8,815 shacks plus brick houses were identified in aerial photos of informal settlements in 2011 and 11,803 in 2016, meaning that over 400 new units were added per year.

FIGURE 3: Increase in Housing Units in Oshakati, 1991-2011

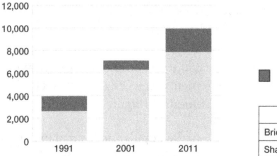

	1991	2001	2011
Bricks	68%	89%	79%
Shacks	32%	11%	21%

Legend: ■ Shacks □ Bricks/blocks

Source: Weber and Mendelsohn (2017: 66)

In Oshakati, informal settlement upgrading has been a priority and, as Figure 4 shows, there have been increases in access to electricity, gas, shared pit/bucket toilets, and private flush toilets. As Weber and Mendelsohn (2017) note: "Oshakati has made concerted efforts to control and upgrade informal settlements. It also has the distinction of allowing people to build permanent homes in informal settlements (which) anticipates the implementation of measures to upgrade those areas without significantly altering their physical structure." This policy has improved the living conditions of many residents of informal settlements.

FIGURE 4: Services in Oshakati, 1991-2011

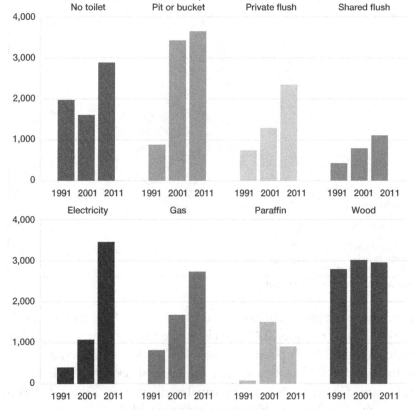

Source: Weber and Mendelsohn (2017: 70)

2.4 Rural-Urban Migration

Rural poverty is a major driver of movement to urban centres in Namibia (Pendleton and Frayne, 1998). The 2009/2010 Namibia Household Income and Expenditure Survey (NHIES) indicated that 27.2% of the rural population were poor compared to 9.5% of the urban. The 2015/2016 NHIES found that the proportion of poor had declined slightly to 25.1% in the rural (compared to 8.6% in the urban). However, the number of people who are severely poor in the urban areas grew from 4.4% in 2009/2010 to 4.8% in 2015/2016. Pendleton and Frayne (1998) showed that in the late 1990s, 33% of urban migrants from the north-west of the country remained unemployed, thus increasing the proportion of urban poor. One-third or more of the urban population in the informal areas were severely poor. With projected urbanization, and assuming no change in rural and urban poverty incidence, half or more of the country's poor will be in urban areas in 20 years' time.

Movement from rural areas to towns in communal areas (such as Oshakati and Ondangwa) is the second largest form of migration in the country (Frayne and Pendleton, 2001). Rapid urbanization in the north has taken place in a context of severe environmental constraints, including natural disasters such as flooding and drought (leading to declining agricultural production) as well as poverty, inequality, and uneven regional development. A high natural population growth rate, population pressure, land degradation, and the lack of or limited rural economic activity have also played key roles (Fuller and Prommer, 2000). Although the north of the country is still predominantly rural, with the population deriving part of its livelihood from subsistence agriculture, the majority supplement their subsistence with non-agricultural activities. Droughts and floods have severely reduced agricultural production, weakening the rural economy in Owamboland. The decline in agricultural production was also precipitated by heavy male outmigration into wage employment in urban areas (Frayne, 2004). It is within this context that migration from the rural areas surrounding the three towns continues.

There is also evidence uncovered in the Namibian Migration Project of step migration from the rural areas to the towns of the north and onward migration to Windhoek at a later stage. Of the 151,000 migrants captured, the second most common type of movement was from Oshakati to Windhoek and the third most common was from Ondangwa to Windhoek (Frayne and Pendleton, 2003). Smaller migration movements from the towns of the north to other small centres such as Grootfontein, Luderitz, Swakopmund, and Tsumeb were also recorded.

2.5 Municipal Governance

As both Oshakati and Ondangwa started off as towns in communal areas, the current town planning/municipalities struggle to introduce appropriate structures and conformity with municipal regulations. Land registration is a particular challenge (van Asperen, 2010). Efforts in the 1990s to develop community associations to represent residents' interests were not very successful (Frayne et al., 2001). The Local Authorities Act 23 of 1992 redefined municipalities and town councils. A municipality is governed by 7-15 members selected from party lists, whereas town councils have 7-12 members, with female representation of five for municipalities and three for town councils. Councillors may serve for three terms. Oshakati, Ongwediva, and Ondangwa are administered by their respective town councils and secretariat. The council is headed by the mayor supported by the deputy mayor and a team of elected members who are from different constituencies within the boundaries of the town. The secretariat is headed by a chief executive officer with various departments headed by directors. The overall function of the town council is to make legally binding policies and decisions and the secretariat provides guidance on implementation. The mandate of the councils is to provide housing, road infrastructure, water and sanitation, and other services to residents.

3. METHODOLOGY

This report provides a picture of the urban food security situation in the Oshakati-Ongwediva-Ondangwa corridor. It assesses the demographic and economic status of households, levels of food insecurity, main sources of food, and frequency of sourcing, dietary quality, the importance of urban agriculture as a source of food, and rural-to-urban informal food transfers. It is based on a household survey conducted in mid-2017 in all three towns. The questionnaire was based on the 2008 AFSUN household baseline survey instrument, which was updated by the Hungry Cities Partnership (HCP) in 2015. The target sample size for the survey was 910 households, based on the following assumptions:

- A precision equal to 95% confidence interval, with a corresponding power of 80%;
- A non-response household rate of 30%;
- A margin of error of 6.5%;
- A conservative design effect of 2.0; and
- A household food insecurity prevalence of 50%.

The proposed sample distribution was 51% for Oshakati, 20% for Ongwediva, and 29% for Ondangwa. The selection of households for interview was based on the following sampling strategy. First, the number of Primary Sampling Units (PSUs) in each town was determined. This was based on probability proportional to size (PPS), which gave a total of 35 PSUs for the three towns: 18 in Oshakati, 7 in Ongwediva and 10 in Ondangwa (Table 2). Second, from each of the selected PSUs, a fixed number of households (26) was calculated to give a total sample size for each town: 468 in Oshakati, 182 in Ongwediva, and 260 in Ondangwa.

TABLE 2: Target Sample Size Per Constituency and Town			
Town	Constituency	No. of PSUs	Proposed no. of sampled households per PSU
Oshakati	Oshakati East	10	26*10 = 260
Oshakati	Oshakati West	8	26*8 = 208
Ongwediva	Ongwediva	7	26*7 = 182
Ondangwa	Ondangwa Urban	10	26*10 = 260
Total		35	910

Maps from the Namibian Statistics Agency (NSA) were used to trace the boundaries of each PSU. A household list was prepared for each PSU and households were identified for interview using systematic random sampling from each list. Student enumerators from the University of Namibia were deployed within each PSU to interview the selected households. Each head of household, or a representative older than 18 years old, was asked to participate in the survey, following the presentation of an introductory letter from the constituency. Because the response rate was lower in Ongwediva, additional households were sampled in Oshakati (Table 3).

TABLE 3: Household Response Rate			
Town	No. of households targeted	No. of households interviewed	Household response rate (%)
Oshakati	468	493	105.3
Ongwediva	182	146	80.2
Ondangwa	260	214	82.3
Total	910	853	93.7

The survey was programmed into tablets using ODK software for ease of administration. Geo-coordinates were captured on the tablets after every interview. The spatial distribution of the sampled households in each town is shown in Figures 5 and 6.

FIGURE 5: Spatial Distribution of Households Surveyed in Oshakati and Ongwediva

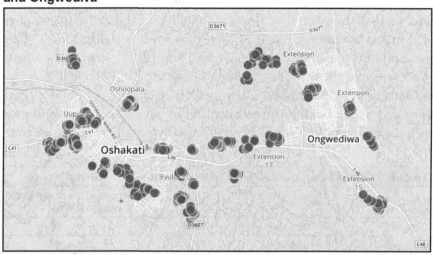

FIGURE 6: Spatial Distribution of Households Surveyed in Ondangwa

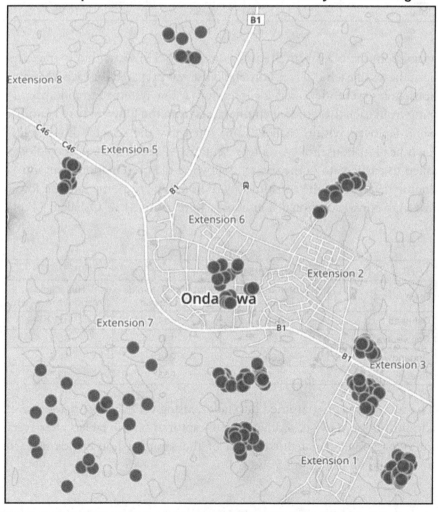

4. HOUSEHOLD CHARACTERISTICS

4.1 Household Size

The average household size in Oshakati, Ongwediva, and Ondangwa was 4.4 with a standard deviation of 3.1. There is considerable variability in household size with one-member households making up about 11% of the sample, 2-4-member households comprising 37%, and one-third having between 5 and 10 members (Figure 7). A few households had more than 10 members.

FIGURE 7: Distribution of Household Size

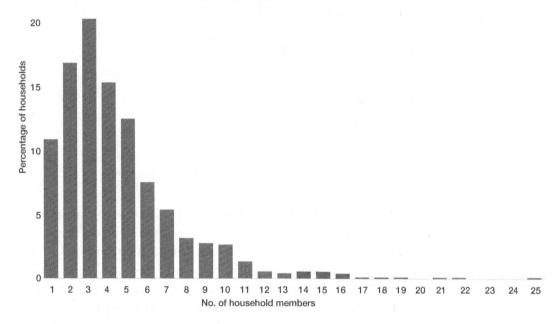

4.2 Age and Sex of Household Members

The age distribution of household members in Oshakati, Ongwediva, and Ondangwa shows that slightly over 50% were below the age of 25 (Figure 8). Children under five years old comprised 13% of the population. Overall, household members of working age (16-60 years) made up two-thirds of the sample. The proportion of people over the age of 60 was relatively small, at only 3%. The age distribution pattern was broadly similar to that observed in a household survey of Windhoek in 2016, although Windhoek had proportionally more children and fewer working-age and elderly people.

FIGURE 8: Comparative Age Distribution of Household Members

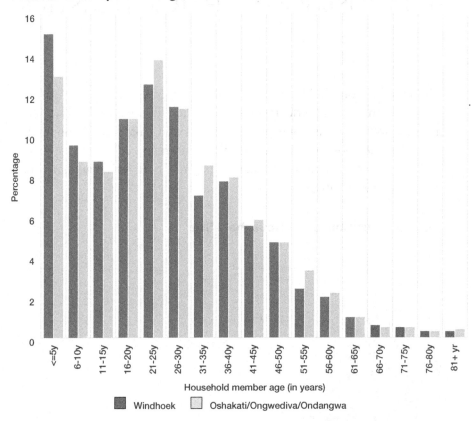

Women outnumbered men by 54% to 46%. This ratio is consistent with data from the 2011 Census which found more women than men in the urban areas of the four constituencies (52% female in Ondangwa Urban, 56% in Ongwediva, 55% in Oshakati East, and 56% in Oshakati West). The gender imbalance is also present in the rural parts of the constituencies with women in the majority. Movement from the rural areas to smaller towns such as Ondangwa and Oshakati has always been dominated by women. In part, this imbalance might be explained by the historical pattern of male migration from the north to Windhoek (Frayne and Pendleton, 2003). However, the 2016 Windhoek survey found that 47% of household members were male and 53% were female. This is a clear break with the past and reflects growing female migration to the capital in recent years (Nickanor, 2014; Nickanor and Kazembe, 2017; Nickanor et al., 2016).

TABLE 4: Gender Balance in Urban and Rural Areas of Constituencies		% female	% male
Ondangwa	Urban	52.3	47.7
	Rural	56.2	46.8
Ongwediva	Urban	55.9	44.1
	Rural	54.4	44.6
Oshakati East	Urban	54.7	45.3
	Rural	54.5	45.5
Oshakati West	Urban	55.9	44.1
	Rural	56.1	43.9

Source: Regional Profiles. Namibia Statistics Agency, 2014

4.3 Migration from Rural Areas

The majority (over 60%) of the household heads were born in rural areas, while only 22% were born in the three towns (Figure 9). Another 11% were born in different towns. Despite the proximity of Angola, only a few household heads (less than 3%) were born outside Namibia. This profile confirms that much of the recent growth of these secondary cities has been driven by in-migration from rural areas. On the other hand, close to half (48%) of all household members were born in the three towns, with the proportion born in rural areas dropping to 41% (Figure 10). This suggests that many household heads who moved to town have remained and their children have been born there. This is confirmed by Table 5, which shows that the average age of household heads born in rural areas is 44, while the average age of other household members born in the three towns is only 16. The table also shows that adult migration from rural areas does not only consist of household heads, as the mean age of other household members born in rural areas is 28.

FIGURE 9: Birthplace of Household Heads

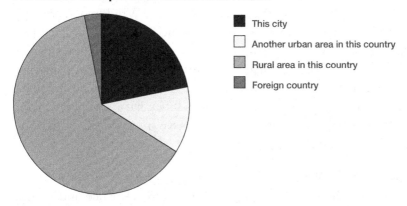

FIGURE 10: Birthplace of Other Household Members

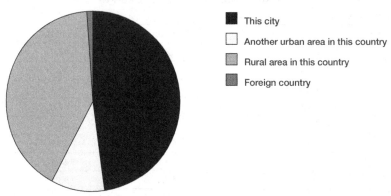

■ This city

☐ Another urban area in this country

▨ Rural area in this country

▨ Foreign country

TABLE 5: Mean Age of Household Heads and Others by Place of Birth		
Place of birth	Head of household	Other members
	Mean age	Mean age
This city	41.2	15.9
Another urban area in Namibia	39.1	19.9
Rural area in Namibia	44.2	27.7
Another country	47.4	35.9
Total	42.9	20.5

4.4 Level of Education

Table 6 shows the education level of all household members and adult household members by the highest level of education attained. The former includes children still at school while the latter focuses only on the adult population. Only 4% of adults have no schooling, while another 14% have some primary education. The largest group (36%) have some high school education, while 23% have completed high school. Around one-quarter of the population have some tertiary education, with 8% having university qualifications and another 8% non–university post–secondary qualifications. In comparing the three towns with Windhoek, it is clear that the capital has a higher proportion of adults with no or little education (28% versus 18% with primary school or lower). The proportion with some high school is similar, while Windhoek has a lower number who have finished high school (14% versus 23%). Both have similar post-secondary education profiles, although Windhoek has more people with post-graduate degrees and the three towns have more people with non-university post-secondary qualifications.

The education level of household members disaggregated by sex and relationship to household heads is provided in Figure 11. Male and female heads have relatively similar educational profiles. The main gender differences are apparent with spouses (where female spouses tend to be better educated), and with sons and daughters (where daughters tend to be better educated).

TABLE 6: Highest Level of Education Attained by Household Members

	Oshakati/Ongwediva/ Ondangwa		Windhoek	
	All household members (%)	Household members over 18 (%)	All household members (%)	Household members over 18 (%)
Level of education				
No formal schooling	14.4	4.0	16.7	6.1
Some primary school	17.8	8.0	24.5	13.6
Primary completed	6.4	5.7	6.8	8.6
Some high school	30.6	35.7	30.8	38.9
High school completed	15.2	22.7	9.2	14.2
Some university	5.3	7.9	5.3	8.1
University completed	5.1	7.9	3.5	5.5
Post-graduate	0.3	0.5	2.3	3.7
Other post-secondary qualification	4.9	7.5	0.9	1.4
N	3,594	2,301	3,758	2,258

FIGURE 11: Education Level by Sex and Relationship to Household Head

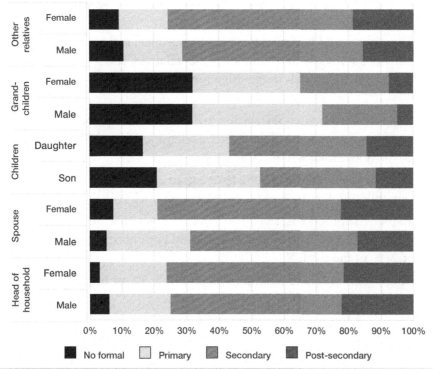

Figure 12 shows the education levels of school-going household members disaggregated by sex. Most children aged 5-12 are in primary school, with a similar percentage of boys and girls. However, more boys aged 13-18 are still in primary school, with proportionately more girls in that age group in high school.

FIGURE 12: Age, Sex and Level of Education of School-Going Household Members

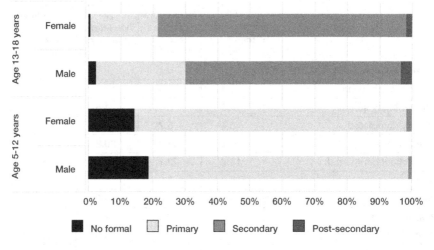

4.5 Types of Household

The household typology used in the survey assigns households to one of five categories:

- Female-centred households with a female head and no husband/male partner but may include children, other relatives, and friends. As many as 40% of households in the three towns were female-centred (Figure 13).

- Male-centred households with a male head and no wife/female partner but may include children, other relatives, and friends. Only 19% of the households fell into this category.

- Nuclear households generally have a head and a partner with or without children. Just 16% of households were nuclear in structure.

- Extended households have a head and a partner plus their children and other relatives. This was the second most common type of household at 21% of the total.

- Single-person households amounted to only 3% of the sample.

FIGURE 13: Household Typology

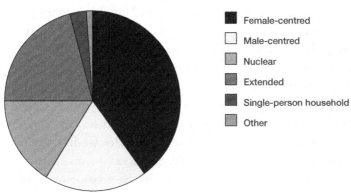

- ■ Female-centred
- □ Male-centred
- ▨ Nuclear
- ▨ Extended
- ■ Single-person household
- ▨ Other

5. Poverty and Livelihoods

5.1 Income Inequality in Namibia

Namibia has been ranked by the World Bank as an upper-middle-income country since 2009. In 2015, the country had an estimated GDP per capita of USD4,902, which is relatively high for a developing country. However, this wealth is highly unequally distributed with a GINI coefficient of 0.597 in 2009/2010 (NSA, 2012). In 2016, the NSA-NHIES classified households that spend less than NAD520.80 per month as poor and those that spend less than NAD389.30 per month as severely poor. The poverty lines for earlier years are shown in Table 7. In addition, a household that spent NAD293.10 or less per month on food in 2016 was classified as food poor. The NSA data shows that between 2003/2004 and 2015/2016 the incidence of poverty nationally fell from 38% to 18%, of severe poverty from 22% to 11%, and of food poverty from 9% to 6%. The reduction in poverty can be attributed to general increases in national income combined with the impact of social grants and other government interventions to reduce poverty through various national development plans.

TABLE 7: Namibia's Poverty Lines (NAD/month)			
Type of poverty line	2003/2004	2009/2010	2015/2016
Food poverty line	127.15	204.05	293.10
Lower-bound poverty line	184.56	277.54	389.30
Upper-bound poverty line	262.45	377.96	520.80
Food poverty line – head count ratio (%)	9.00	7.30	5.80
Lower-bound poverty line – head count ratio (%)	21.90	15.30	11.00
Upper-bound poverty line – head count ratio (%)	37.70	28.70	18.00
Source: NSA-NHIES 2015/2016: Key Poverty Indicators			

While the incidence of poverty and severe poverty has declined over time, acute inequalities in the distribution of income in Namibia remain as an apartheid legacy, and much of the population continues to live in poverty. Indeed, inequality in Namibia is among the highest in the world. Poverty has always been particularly severe among female-centred households (Nickanor, 2014; Pendleton et al., 2012). Figure 14 suggests that in the three towns combined, 5% of households are severely poor, 9% are marginally poor, and only 3% are food poor. Oshakati has the highest levels of poverty, followed by Ondangwa and then Ongwediva. As this report shows, these official metrics and estimates of food poverty seriously underestimate the prevalence of food insecurity in the urbanizing north.

FIGURE 14: Income Poverty Levels

5.2 Housing Type

Houses are the most common type of dwelling of surveyed households in the three towns (at 38%), followed by shacks (34%), and townhouses (11%) (Table 8). Other dwellings included flats/apartment and traditional homesteads, although these made up less than 10% each. Although there is no necessary correlation between housing type and level of poverty, the one-third of the sample living in shacks in informal settlements are likely to be in the poorest section of the population. However, as noted above, informal settlements contain both shacks and brick houses.

TABLE 8: Types of Dwelling		
	No.	%
House	322	38.1
Shack in informal settlement	287	34.0
Townhouse	94	11.1
Flat/apartment	66	7.8
Traditional dwelling/homestead	42	5.0
Backyard shack attached to house	13	1.5
Room in house	7	0.8

Room in flat	1	0.1
Hotel/boarding house	1	0.1
Other	12	1.4
Total	845	100

5.3 Household Income

Children of school-going age, plus pre-schoolers and youths including students, constitute 47% of the household population (Figure 15). Of the rest, around 20% (and 31% of adults aged 18 and above) work full-time, while 9% (and 14% of adults) are self-employed. Smaller numbers are in part-time and/or seasonal work – 4% and 7% respectively. While the percentages in full-time and part-time work are similar in Windhoek, the capital had lower numbers of self-employed and higher unemployment than the three towns.

FIGURE 15: Work Status of Household Members

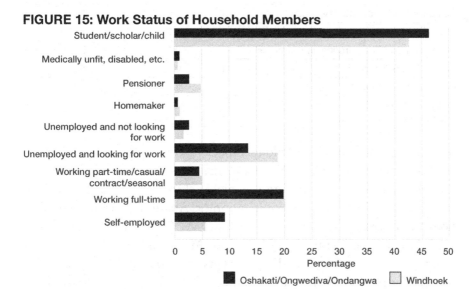

Formal wage work is the principal income source for more than half the surveyed households in the towns (at 53%) (Table 9). Other sources include grants and income from the sale of goods (both 11% of households), casual work (10%), informal work (10%), and cash remittances (9%). Table 9 also gives the average amount of income received from each source. Formal wage work provided an average of NAD10,294 per month, which is considerably higher than all other sources of income. Informal sector activities generated amounts from an average NAD1,433 per month for renting property to NAD2,852 for selling fresh produce not produced by the household. The one in every 10 households receiving remittances got an average of NAD1,530 per month. A similar proportion getting social grants received an average of NAD1,309 per month.

TABLE 9: Sources of Household Income

	% of households	Average monthly amount (NAD)
Formal wage work	53.1	10,294
Income from informal business (sale of goods)	11.4	2,499
Government social grants	11.0	1,309
Casual wage work	10.2	1,726
Informal wage work	9.8	2,401
Cash remittances	8.6	1,530
Income from formal business	6.5	9,955
Income from informal sale of fresh produce produced by household	4.5	2,313
Income from informal sale of fresh produce not produced by household	4.1	2,852
Income from informal renting of property	1.8	1,433
Other informal income	1.5	2,846
Gifts	1.2	1,183
Informal loans from moneylenders	0.6	2,720
Non-government formal grants or aid	0.2	4,600
Interest earned on personal investments	0.1	3,000
Formal bank loans	0.1	15,000
Other income source	2.1	2,185

Note: Multiple-response question
1USD = NAD13.7 (2016)

The average monthly household income is NAD6,912. However, a standard deviation of NAD9,946 and a median income of only NAD2,900 indicates that income distribution is highly skewed. This is also evident in Table 10, which shows income quintiles. About 41% of the sampled households have a monthly income below NAD2,100 and 60% of households have an income below NAD4,200. An income of NAD2,100 per month works out to about USD2.4 per person per day, indicating extreme poverty for more than 40% of the households in Oshakati, Ongwediva, and Ondangwa. The 20% of households that earn between NAD2,101 and NAD4,200 are still poor. Even an income of NAD10,000 per month (or NAD120,000 per year) does not signify wealth when the official basic-needs basket costs NAD10,661 per month.

TABLE 10: Income Quintiles

	No.	%	Cumulative %
1 (<=NAD1,100)	159	23.3	23.3
2 (NAD1,101-NAD2,100)	118	17.3	40.6
3 (NAD2,101-NAD4,200)	133	19.5	60.1
4 (NAD4,201-NAD12,000)	149	21.8	81.9
5 (NAD12,001+)	124	18.1	100.0
Total	683	100.0	

5.4 Household Expenditure

Virtually all of the sampled households purchased food and groceries and nearly three-quarters paid for public utilities such as water, sanitation, and electricity in the month prior to the survey (Figure 16). Other common expenditures included transportation (61% of households), telecommunications (58%), and fuel (41%). Around one-quarter spent funds on housing, the informal purchase of utilities, and medical care. Only 14% spent income on education. As many as one-third of households were able to save money and 27% sent remittances to rural areas. This is a much larger figure than the number of households receiving remittances from other parts of the country (9%). Table 11 provides additional information on average household expenditure in each category. Although most households spent on food and groceries, and utilities, the average amounts were relatively low compared to other types of expenditure. For example, the average monthly spend on food and groceries was NAD921, while NAD576 was spent on public utilities.

FIGURE 16: Expenses Incurred by Households

Larger average expenditures included housing, insurance, furniture, and clothing, although, as noted, the number of households with these expenditures was much lower. Interestingly, the highest expenditures were on financial transactions including debt repayment and savings. Remittances sent to rural areas were close to half the amounts received from outside the area (NAD881 versus NAD1,530). Comparing expenditure patterns with Windhoek, more households in the Oshakati-Ondangwa-Ongwediva corridor spent on virtually all line items (with the exception of housing and education). Levels of savings and remitting are also higher in the three towns. A key question is whether the savings levels indicate that households meet their dietary needs and are food secure.

TABLE 11: Household Expenditure Average Amounts		
	% of house-holds	Average monthly amount (NAD)
Food and groceries	99.1	921
Public utilities (water, electricity, sanitation)	71.4	576
Transportation	60.8	463
Telecommunications (cell-phone, telephone, internet)	58.1	197
Fuel (firewood, charcoal, paraffin, kerosene, propane)	40.5	221
Savings	33.5	1,808
Cash remittances to rural areas	26.7	881
Housing (rent, mortgage payments, maintenance, renovation)	25.7	1,443
Informally purchased utilities (water, electricity, sanitation)	23.0	198
Medical care	22.4	466
Donations, gifts	19.1	848
Clothing	18.9	1,216
Education (tuition, books, uniforms)	13.6	910
Insurance	11.4	1,350
Household furniture, tools and appliances	9.1	1,315
Entertainment	8.2	501
Debt repayments	3.9	1,874
Note: Multiple-response question		

5.5 Lived Poverty

The Lived Poverty Index (LPI) is a well-tested subjective measure of poverty. An LPI score for each household is derived from answers to a set of questions on how often it has gone without certain basic needs in the previous year including food, medical attention, cooking fuel, and cash income. Responses are measured on a five-point Likert scale: never, just once or twice, several times, many times, and always. A mean LPI score is computed for each of these basic needs. A mean score closer to 0 indicates fewer households "going without", while a score closer to 4 suggests more households "going without".

As Figure 17 shows, nearly three-quarters of the households had an LPI of 1.00 or less. Of the rest, one-quarter scored between 1.01 and 2.00. A much smaller number (11%) scored more than 2.01. The mean LPI score for the entire sample was 0.88 (median = 0.67), which was much lower than the mean of 1.78 (median = 2.0) in the equivalent study of Windhoek. This means that households in Oshakati, Ongwediva, and Ondangwa have lower levels of lived poverty, on average, than those in Windhoek. This is confirmed by the comparative distribution of LPI scores in Figure 17.

FIGURE 17: Lived Poverty Index

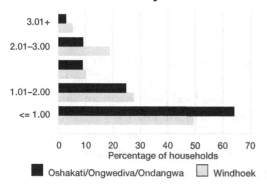

There were marked differences in the LPI scores between the three towns, which varied from 1.01 in Oshakati to 0.88 in Ondangwa to 0.55 in Ongwediva (Table 12). The level of lived poverty is therefore markedly higher in Oshakati. With a standard deviation of 0.96, inequality in lived poverty is also greatest in Oshakati. These differences are captured in Figure 18, which shows that over 40% of households in Oshakati had an LPI of more than 1.01, compared to 37% in Ondangwa and only 24% in Ongwediva.

TABLE 12: Average Lived Poverty Index by Town			
	Lived Poverty Index		
	Mean	Median	Standard deviation
Oshakati	1.01	0.83	0.96
Ongwediva	0.55	0.33	0.70
Ondangwa	0.88	0.66	0.89
Total	0.89	0.67	0.91

FIGURE 18: Distribution of Lived Poverty Index Scores by Town

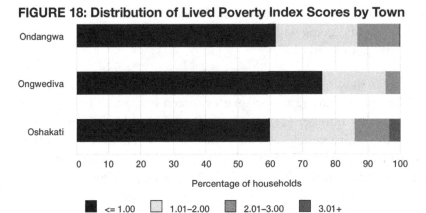

6. HOUSEHOLD FOOD SECURITY

6.1 Measuring Household Food Insecurity

The FAO defines food security as a situation where "all people, at all times, have physical and economic access to sufficient safe and nutritious food that meets their dietary needs and food preferences for an active and healthy life." This definition highlights four key food security dimensions: the need for sufficient food to be available, an ability to access that food, that the foods that are accessed contribute to the nutritional status of the household (utilization), and the need for access to that food "at all times" (stability).

The study used four measures of food security that have been developed, tested, and refined by the Food and Nutrition Technical Assistance (FANTA) project over many years:

- Household Food Insecurity Access Scale (HFIAS): The HFIAS score is a continuous measure of the degree of food insecurity in the household (Coates et al., 2007). An HFIAS score is calculated for each household based on answers to nine frequency-of-occurrence questions designed to capture different components of the household experience of food insecurity in the previous four weeks. The minimum score is 0 and the maximum is 27. The higher the score, the more food insecurity the household experienced. The lower the score, the less food insecurity the household experienced.

- Household Food Insecurity Access Prevalence (HFIAP) indicator: The HFIAP indicator is based on the HFIAS and uses a scoring algorithm to categorize households into four levels of household food insecurity: food secure, mildly food insecure, moderately food insecure, and severely food insecure (Coates et al., 2007). Households are categorized as increasingly food insecure as they respond affirmatively to more severe conditions and/or experience those conditions more frequently.

- Household Dietary Diversity Score (HDDS): Dietary diversity refers to how many food groups were consumed within the household in the previous 24 hours (Swindale and Bilinsky 2005). The scale runs from 0 to 12 and a score is calculated for each household. An increase in the average number of different food groups consumed provides a quantifiable measure of improved household dietary diversity.

- Months of Adequate Household Food Provisioning (MAHFP) indicator: The MAHFP indicator captures changes in the household's ability to ensure that food is available above a minimum level all year round (Bilinsky and Swindale, 2010). Households are asked to identify in which months (during the past 12 months) they did not have access to sufficient food to meet their household needs.

6.2 Household Food Insecurity Access

The detailed responses to the nine HFIAS questions addressing household consumption in the previous month are shown in Figure 19. About half indicated that they sometimes/often worry about not having enough food. Just over one-third had eaten smaller meals and 42% had eaten fewer meals because there was not enough food in the house, which suggests that these worries were justified. A smaller number (20%) said there was sometimes or often no food in the house. A similar number (22%) said that household members had gone to bed hungry at night. Slightly fewer had gone a whole day or night without eating because there was no food in the house.

A second set of questions concerns the quality of household diet. Over 40% of the households had eaten a limited variety of food due to a lack of resources. A similar proportion had eaten foods that they did not want to due to an inability to purchase those they preferred. Finally, close to half of the households sometimes missed out on the foods they preferred due to a lack of resources. In general, it appears that food insecurity manifests more in terms of the quality of the food consumed than an absolute shortage of food. However, a significant minority do experience absolute shortages, which leads to coping behaviours such as eating fewer and smaller meals.

FIGURE 19: Frequency of Experience of Food Insecurity in Previous Month

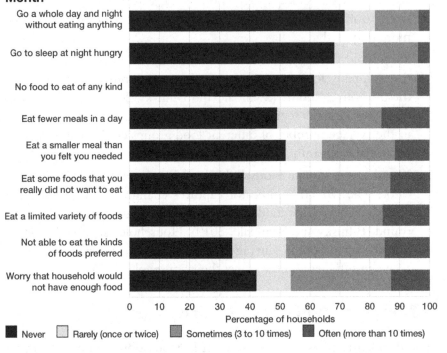

The HFIAS scores derived from this data show that almost half of the sampled households had a low HFIAS score of 6 or less, indicating lower levels of food insecurity (Table 13). However, one-quarter had very high HFIAS scores of 12 or more. Close to 13% of the households had scores over 15. A comparison of the HFIAS distribution with that for Windhoek shows very clearly that households in Windhoek are the more food insecure (Figure 20). For example, 35% of households in the three towns had scores of 3 or less, compared with only 23% in Windhoek. At the other end of the food security spectrum, 53% of Windhoek households had HFIAS scores of 12 or more compared with 30% of the town households.

TABLE 13: Frequency Distribution of Household HFIAS			
HFIAS range	No.	%	Cumulative %
<=3.00	290	34.7	34.7
3.01-6.00	109	13.1	47.8
6.01-9.00	91	10.9	58.7
9.01-12.00	92	11.0	69.7
12.01-15.00	66	7.9	77.6
15.01-18.00	80	9.6	87.2
18.01-21.00	54	6.5	93.7
21.01-24.00	35	4.2	97.8
24.01-27.00	18	2.2	100.0
Total	835		

FIGURE 20: Comparison of Food Security in Oshakati-Ongwediva-Ondangwa with Windhoek

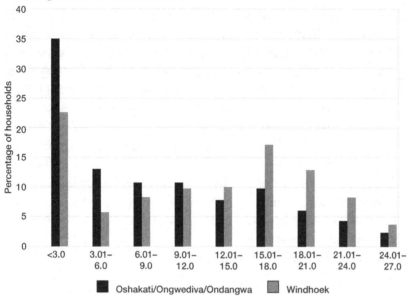

6.3 Household Food Insecurity Access Prevalence

The HFIAP groups households into four main food security categories and gives greater precision to the HFIAS findings. Just over half (52%) of the households in the corridor fall into the severely food insecure category and only 23% are completely food secure (Table 14). Combining the moderately and severely food insecure into a single "food insecure" category would mean that nearly 70% of households experience a significant degree of food insecurity. A comparison with Windhoek, however, suggests that while overall levels of food insecurity are high, the situation is not as bad as in the capital. There, only 16% of households are completely food secure and 67% are severely food insecure, with 80% experiencing a significant degree of food insecurity.

TABLE 14: Comparative HFIAP Distribution				
HFIAP	Oshakati-Ondangwa-Ongwediva		Windhoek	
	No.	%	No.	%
Food secure	194	22.9	141	16.4
Mildly food insecure	71	8.4	29	3.4
Moderately food insecure	147	17.3	113	13.1
Severely food insecure	437	51.5	577	67.1
Total	849	100.0	860	100.0

6.4 Household Dietary Diversity

The HDDS captures the number of food groups eaten in the household in the previous 24 hours, with a maximum score of 12 and a minimum of 0. The mean HDDS was 4.8, indicating that food from less than five food groups was consumed by the average household. Nearly 20% of the households had an HDDS of 2 or less and two-thirds had an HDDS of 5 or less. By comparison, the mean HDDS score in Windhoek was 3.2, indicating that urban households in the capital have an even less diverse diet than those in the north. This is confirmed by the frequency distribution of households shown in Table 15, where two-thirds of Windhoek households have an HDDS of 3 or less, compared with only one-third of households in the north. Similarly, 89% of Windhoek households have an HDDS of 5 or less compared with 65% in the north. The northern towns are even better off in terms of dietary diversity: for example, 22% have an HDDS of 7 or more compared with only 7% in Windhoek.

HDDS score	Oshakati-Ongwediva-Ondangwa		Windhoek	
	%	Cumulative %	%	Cumulative %
0	1.0	1.0	2.2	2.2
1	2.6	3.6	6.8	9.0
2	15.5	19.1	39.3	48.3
3	12.2	31.3	17.7	66.0
4	14.0	45.4	13.5	79.4
5	19.8	65.2	9.7	89.1
6	12.4	77.6	3.6	92.7
7	9.5	87.0	3.2	95.9
8	6.0	93.0	2.0	97.9
9	4.3	97.4	1.4	99.3
10	1.2	98.6	0.4	99.6
11	1.0	99.5	0.2	99.9
12	0.5	100.0	0.1	100.0
Total	100.0		100.0	

TABLE 15: Comparison of Household Dietary Diversity Scores

In terms of the actual food groups consumed, non-nutritive foodstuffs (such as sugar and tea/coffee) are consumed by most households. If these are removed from the analysis, the dietary diversity scores are even lower in both parts of the country. Cereals (in the form of *mahangu*, maize and sorghum) are a dietary staple and are consumed by 96% of households (Figure 21). As many as 58% of households in the northern towns supplemented their cereal with meat and nearly half with fish. The consumption of vegetables, fruit, and dairy was significantly lower.

Table 16 compares the situation in the north with Windhoek and explains why dietary diversity scores are much lower in Windhoek. More households in the Oshakati, Ongwediva, and Ondangwa sample consumed food from every food group than the Windhoek households. The most significant differences were fish (40% versus 5%), vegetables (32% versus 21%), and fruit (20% versus 5%). The main reason is that the northern households are closer to communal production, closer to wild fruits like *eembe* and *makalani*, and fish is available during the rainy season in the *oshanas*.

FIGURE 21: Consumption of Different Food Groups

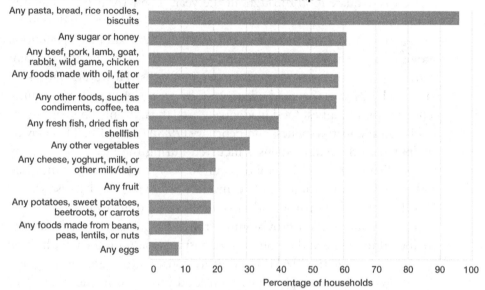

TABLE 16: Comparison of Food Groups Consumed

	% of households in Oshakati-Ongwediva-Ondangwa	% of households in Windhoek
Any pasta, bread, rice noodles, biscuits or any other foods made from flour, millet, sorghum, maize, rice, wheat, or oats	95.6	94.2
Any sugar or honey	61.3	34.0
Any beef, pork, lamb, goat, rabbit, wild game, chicken, duck, other birds, chicken heads and feet, liver, kidney, heart, or other organ meats/offal	57.5	49.8
Any foods made with oil, fat, or butter	57.2	29.5
Any other foods, such as condiments, coffee, tea	56.8	26.5
Any fresh fish, dried fish, or shellfish	39.9	4.6
Any cheese, yoghurt, milk, or other milk/dairy products	20.9	14.6
Any fruit	19.5	5.4
Any potatoes, sweet potatoes, beetroots, carrots, or any other foods made from them	18.3	11.6

Any other vegetables	-	31.5	20.8
Any foods made from beans, peas, lentils, or nuts		16.2	6.0
Any eggs		8.3	5.3

6.5 Months of Adequate Household Food Provisioning

Seasonality of food supply is a critical aspect of food and nutrition in Namibia. For a household to be deemed fully food secure, it should have access to adequate food throughout the year. The MAHFP is a measure of the seasonality of food insecurity where households are asked to identify any months in the previous year in which they had inadequate food provisioning. On average, the sampled households in the three towns had adequate food provisioning for 10.8 months. However, only 43% of households said they had adequate food provisioning all year round. The months of highest food inadequacy are January (only 63% of households had adequate supplies) and February (79%) (Table 17). This may be attributed to the extra expenses incurred during the December holiday season. From April to December, over 90% of households said they had sufficient food provisioning. The months following the harvest season (April to July) show particularly low levels of food inadequacy. There is a slight decline in food provisioning from July onwards, which may be attributed to saving and rationalizing consumption until the next harvest season. In general, the MAHFP scores are consistently high, showing that these towns do not simply depend on food produced in the immediate city-region. Most foods (including cereals) are brought in from elsewhere in the country, or from South Africa by the supermarkets, and are available throughout the year for purchase.

TABLE 17: Monthly Distribution of Food Adequacy		
	No.	% of households
January	527	62.7
February	666	79.3
March	753	89.6
April	759	90.4
May	775	92.3
June	813	96.8
July	816	97.1
August	785	93.5
September	799	95.1
October	804	95.7
November	805	95.8
December	791	94.2

6.6 Impact of Food Price Increases

Rising food costs generally have a significant negative impact on household food security as they affect access and utilization of food. As prices rise, households find it more difficult to afford a basic food basket. Poor households are disproportionately affected and may experience a drop in the amount of food they consume as well as decreased dietary diversity. Figure 22 shows that only 29% of households in the northern towns felt no impact from food price rises. Of the rest, 30% felt the impact monthly (probably when they went shopping for staples in bulk) and 40% on a weekly basis or even more frequently.

FIGURE 22: Frequency of Experience of Impact of Food Price Changes

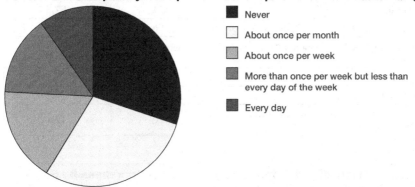

- ■ Never
- □ About once per month
- ▨ About once per week
- ▨ More than once per week but less than every day of the week
- ■ Every day

Table 18 shows which food types were most affected by price changes by showing the proportion of households that went without foods of a particular type due to their unaffordability. Meat products were deemed to be the most unaffordable (by 83% of households), followed by cereals (69%), potatoes (69%), eggs (50%), vegetables (47%), and dairy products (43%). There were no food types that no households found unaffordable. Overall, these responses suggest that rising food prices affect household food accessibility, dietary diversity, and the consumption of more nutritious foods.

Table 19 shows a strong association between food price changes and household food insecurity. The more food insecure a household is, the higher the probability of it being negatively affected by food price increases. In the sample, only 29% of households were never affected by food price increases. Of these, 60% were food secure and 13% were severely food insecure. The majority of food secure households said they were never affected by food price increases, and those that were had experienced this relatively infrequently (about once per month when buying staples). On the other hand, less than 10% of the severely food insecure said they were never affected.

TABLE 18: Food Groups Deemed Unaffordable

	No. of households	% of households that went without due to food prices
Any beef, pork, lamb, goat, rabbit, wild game, chicken, duck, other birds, chicken heads and feet, or offal	493	83.1
Any pasta, bread, rice noodles, biscuits, or any other foods made from grains	410	69.1
Any potatoes, sweet potatoes, beetroot, carrots, or any other foods made from them	409	69.0
Any other vegetables	276	46.5
Any eggs	294	49.6
Any cheese, yoghurt, milk, or other milk/dairy products	255	43.0
Any fruit	221	37.3
Any foods made with oil, fat, or butter	166	28.0
Any foods made from beans, peas, lentils, or nuts	163	27.5
Any fresh or dried fish or shellfish	131	22.1
Any sugar or honey	114	19.2
Any other foods such as condiments, coffee, tea	72	12.1

TABLE 19: Households Affected by Food Price Increases by Food Insecurity Category

HFIAP category	Never	About once per month	About once per week	More than once per week	Every day
Food secure	60.1	12.1	2.1	3.4	4.9
Mildly food insecure	10.3	10.1	9.7	0.8	6.2
Moderately food insecure	16.2	23.0	11.0	14.4	18.5
Severely food insecure	13.4	54.8	77.2	81.4	70.4
Total	100.0	100.0	100.0	100.0	100.0

6.7 Food Shocks

This section considers internal and external shocks that prevented households in the three towns from having enough food in the six months prior to the survey. Figure 23 provides a list of potential shocks and shows how many households had experienced each. The loss of or reduced employment for a household member was the highest reported shock (experienced by 22% of households), followed by reduced income of a household member (17%). All other shocks were experienced by 10% or fewer households.

FIGURE 23: Experience of Food Shocks

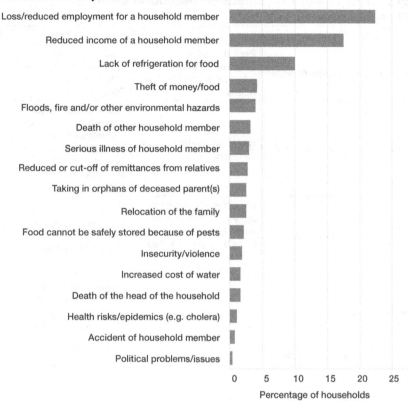

Less than 10% of households said they had experienced environmental shocks in the six months prior to the survey. The timing of the survey may partially explain this as frequent floods have affected households. Tshilunga (2014) notes that there was severe flooding in 2007-2008, 2009-2010, and 2011 and examines the impact of the 2011 floods in northern Namibia on households in the Oshoopala informal settlement in Oshakati. The effects of the floods are summarized in Table 20. With regard to food security "people did not have proper cooking facilities; they used wet wood to cook outside where it was raining most of the time. In most cases, they failed to cook anything in these conditions. As a result, they went without food when it was wet. To others, food stocks were lost in the floods and they were left to starve" (Tshilunga, 2014: 58). As well as destroying urban gardens, the floods affected the livelihoods of traders in the informal food sector and therefore household incomes.

TABLE 20: Impact of 2011 Floods on Oshoopala Informal Settlement, Oshakati

General source	Hazard	Factors	Effects
Poor drainage	Stagnant water	Poor drainage Shallow, hand-dug informal drains between houses	Health concerns (children play in unhygienic water) Food limitations
Poor drainage	Surface runoff	Hardened surfaces such as roads	Health concerns (waste deposited into dwellings and related costs) Damage to structures Damage and loss of assets as well as documents
Structural problems	Landscape	Structures in close proximity to wetlands and water bodies Poor building materials Home foundations below ground level	Damage to property Illnesses Missed school and work
Flood exposure	Stagnant water	As above	Homes destroyed Damage to property Downturn of business Community isolation Starvation and hunger

Source: Tshilunga (2014: 64-65)

6.8 Food Insecurity and Household Income

Research in Windhoek has shown that changes in household income, particularly among low-income families, are associated with increased risk of food insecurity (Pendleton et al., 2012; Nickanor, 2016, 2017). Table 21 shows the relationship between the food security indicators and household income for different income quintiles in Oshakati, Ongwediva, and Ondangwa. Lower household incomes are clearly associated with worse food security outcomes. The HFIAS declines from a high mean score of 12.8 for households in the lowest-income quintile to 4.3 for those in the upper-income quintile. Similarly, the HDDS increases from 3.6 to 6.5, and the MAHFP from 10.1 to 11.4. All three indicators therefore suggest that low-income households have the highest levels of food insecurity, and that food security improves as household income increases.

TABLE 21: Food Insecurity Indicators and Household Income

	Income quintiles				
	1	2	3	4	5
HFIAS	12.8	10.3	9.3	7.6	4.3
HDDS	3.6	4.1	4.3	5.3	6.5
MAHFP	10.1	10.5	10.9	11.1	11.4

6.9 Food Insecurity and Household Type

This section of the report examines whether there is any relationship between food insecurity and type of household in the three towns. Nuclear households had the highest HFIAS and extended households the lowest (Table 22). Unlike in Windhoek, there was no significant difference between female-centred and other types of household. Dietary diversity was lowest for male-centred households and highest for extended households. The third measure of food insecurity is the months of adequate household food provisioning. Here again, nuclear households have the lowest (worst) score and extended households the best. These results do not suggest a consistent pattern of food insecurity by household type. The MAHFP scores are similar, which indicates that the causes of food shortage are similar for all households over the course of the year. Nuclear households are more likely to experience food shortages than male and female-centred households, but better dietary diversity for reasons that are unclear. In general, female-centred households are not more food insecure than other types of household.

TABLE 22: Food Insecurity and Household Structure			
Household structure	HFIAS	HDDS	MAHFP
Female-centred	8.8	4.7	10.7
Male-centred	8.7	4.4	10.9
Nuclear	10.1	5.0	10.6
Extended	7.1	5.2	11.1

7. HOUSEHOLD FOOD SOURCES

7.1 Market Sources

Households in Oshakati, Ongwediva, and Ondangwa obtain their food from a variety of sources. South African supermarkets (Pick n Pay, Spar, Shoprite Checkers, Shoprite USave, and Woolworths) have a growing presence in Namibia (Emongor, 2008; Nickanor et al., 2017). Shoprite, Spar, and Pick n Pay have expanded to the smallest towns in Namibia, as has Woermann Brock, which is the only competitive Namibian supermarket. Supermarkets are patronized by virtually all households, followed by markets (56%), small shops (47%), and street vendors (23%) (Figure 24). Oshakati has one planned open market with space for 200 traders, many of whom sell foodstuffs (Kakwambi, 2012). Only 10% of households purchase food from spazas/tuck shops. This pattern is similar to that of Windhoek where 97% of households shop at supermarkets, 50% at markets and 29% from street vendors. The main differences lie in the patronage of small shops (such as grocers, butcheries, and bakeries), which are much less important in the north, and spazas/tuck shops, which are more important in the north. In general, the similarities in supermarket patronage confirm that Namibia's supermarket revolution extends to the north of the country (Nickanor et al., 2017).

Figure 25 shows the frequency with which households obtain their food from each of these sources. Supermarket shopping is predominantly a monthly activity with 70% of households engaged in this pattern. The majority of market shoppers tend to patronize these outlets once per month. Small shops, spazas/tuck shops, and street vendors are patronized much more frequently.

FIGURE 24: Household Food Sources

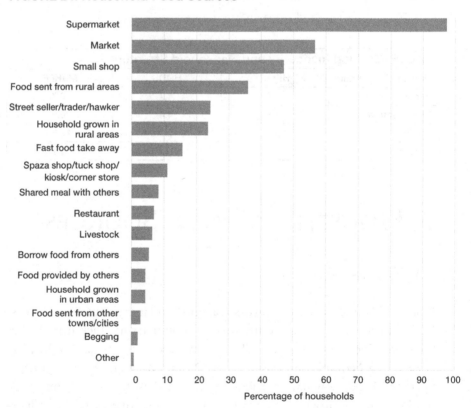

FIGURE 25: Frequency of Food Patronage by Source

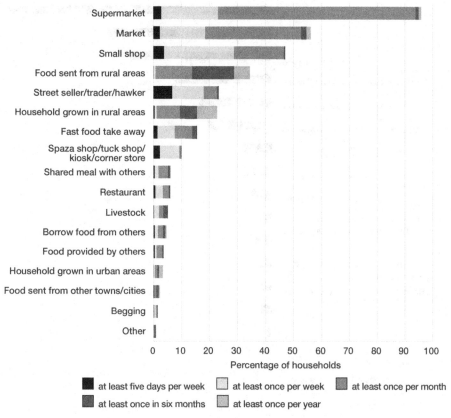

7.2 Food Sourcing and Food Insecurity

By comparing the shopping patterns of food secure and food insecure households, it is possible to determine whether levels of food security influence the sources patronized. Figure 26 shows that food insecure households are just as likely as food secure households to source food from supermarkets. However, food insecure households are more likely to source food from markets (60% versus 46%) and street vendors (26% versus 13%). Food secure households are more likely to source food from small shops (69% versus 51%) and restaurants (36% versus 10%).

7.3 Reasons for Supermarket Patronage

Most households that source food from supermarkets indicated that the food is of better quality, that supermarkets have greater variety of foods, and that they can buy in bulk (Figure 27). Opinion was divided on whether food was cheaper at supermarkets with one-third in agreement and around 40% disagreeing.

FIGURE 26: Food Sources and Food Security Status

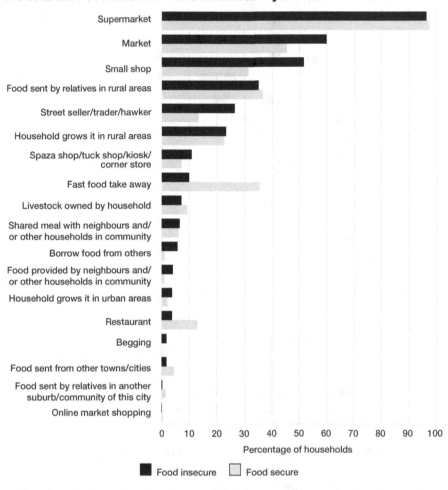

FIGURE 27: Reasons for Shopping at Supermarkets

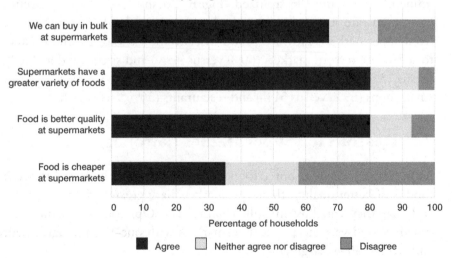

7.4 Purchasing of Different Food Items

The Hungry Cities Food Purchases Matrix (HCFPM) captures how many households purchase a range of common food items and where these items are bought (Crush and McCordic, 2017). The first column in Table 23 shows all food items purchased by at least 20% of households over the previous month. Supermarkets are clearly the dominant source for all food items listed. Over two-thirds of households purchase staple food items such as maize meal, cooking oil, sugar, rice, and pasta from supermarkets. Meat is sourced from a variety of outlets including formal and informal markets and tuck shops, but supermarkets are still the major source. Some households obtain their bread from small shops but, again, supermarkets are the dominant source. Figure 28 shows the proportion of all households that shop for an item by source. Here the dominance of supermarkets is even more apparent.

TABLE 23: Food Items Purchased by Source								
	% of house-holds buying item	Super-market	Small shop	Formal market	Infor-mal market	Tuck shop	Street seller	Other
Cooking oil	88.2	84.3	2.9	0.8	0.1	0.1		
Maize meal	79.6	74.2	3.5	1.6	0.3			
Sugar	75.7	72.3	2.6	0.5	0.2		0.1	
Rice	71.5	68.5	1.6	0.5	0.1	0.4		
Pasta	65.2	64.0	0.9	0.2	0.1			
Fresh meat	58.0	36.5	0.9	6.6	9.7	3.5	0.4	
Tea/coffee	54.7	53.6	0.9	0.1			0.1	
Fresh fish	43.5	13.6	10.7	8.9	1.9	0.5	6.7	1.1
Bread	42.8	30.2	8.7	0.4	0.8	1.9	0.8	
Frozen chicken	34.8	30.0	0.7	1.7	0.7		0.3	
Vegetables	27.7	25.2	0.9	1.4		0.5	0.7	
Frozen fish	24.3	4.4	7.3	8.7	0.5		3.4	
Eggs	23.1	21.3	0.5	0.2	0.1	0.4	0.6	
Fresh milk	23.0	22.5		0.4			0.1	
Pies/ samosa/ vetkoek	22.7	12.5	4.6	1.0	2.1	2.5		
Snacks	21.9	17.0	1.4	0.1	0.2	2.7	0.5	
Fresh fruit	21.5	18.9	0.7	0.6	0.4	0.6	1.3	

FIGURE 28: Proportion of Households Purchasing Items at Different Sources

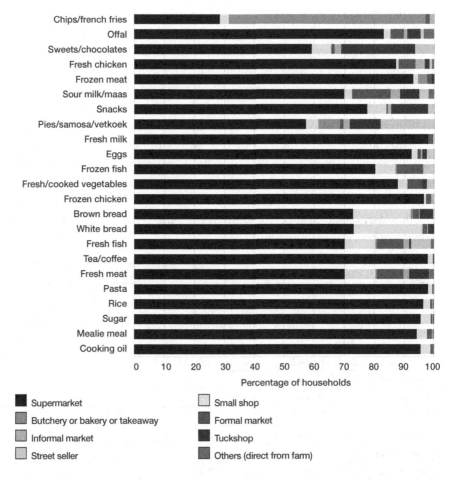

Table 24 shows the frequency with which items are purchased. Cooking oil, maize meal, sugar, rice, pasta, and tea/coffee all tend to be purchased once per month. Most other items are purchased more frequently, although products such as fresh and frozen fish, fresh and frozen meat, frozen chicken, vegetables, snacks, and sour milk are bought only once per month. The only product that most households purchase on a weekly or daily basis is bread.

The households were grouped into food insecure (combining the HFIAP categories of severely and moderately food insecure) and secure (combining mildly food insecure and food secure categories) (Figure 29). Although the differences are not stark, food insecure households tend to purchase fresh items more regularly than food secure households. This is probably because most food insecure households have limited or irregular income and they also may not be able to afford refrigeration.

TABLE 24: Frequency of Purchase of Food Items

	Frequency of purchase (%)			
	At least five days per week	At least once per week	At least twice per month	At least once per month
Bread	26.9	49.3	15.6	8.2
Pies/samosa/vetkoek	19.1	19.1	13.4	48.5
Cooked fish	18.8	25.0	31.3	25.0
Sweets/chocolate	18.5	27.2	28.3	26.1
Cooked meat	14.8	22.2	29.6	33.3
Cooked chicken	11.1	16.7	38.9	33.3
Snacks	9.6	15.0	15.0	60.4
Chips/French fries	9.0	43.3	35.8	11.9
Dried fish	5.0	31.7	21.7	41.7
Fresh fish	4.9	17.0	31.4	46.8
Fresh fish	4.9	17.0	31.4	46.8
Dried vegetables	3.1	21.9	37.5	37.5
Frozen fish	2.9	14.6	33.5	49.0
Frozen fish	2.9	14.6	33.5	49.0
Fresh fruit	2.6	21.6	33.2	42.6
Sour milk/*omaere*	2.6	7.7	33.3	56.4
Offal	2.3	6.8	43.2	47.7
Fresh/cooked vegetables	2.0	13.1	28.2	56.7
Fresh meat	1.4	16.8	39.2	42.6
Fresh milk	1.0	11.2	40.6	47.2
Fresh chicken	0.8	8.7	41.3	49.2
Frozen meat	0.8	9.4	29.1	60.6
Frozen chicken	0.7	8.1	32.0	59.3
Frozen chicken	0.7	8.1	32.0	59.3
Sugar	0.5	3.2	12.2	84.1
Rice	0.5	2.8	11.7	85.0
Pasta	0.5	2.7	9.9	86.8
Eggs	0.5	8.6	34.0	56.9
Tea/coffee	0.4	0.4	12.6	86.5
Cooking oil	0.3	3.1	14.9	81.8
Maize meal	0.1	2.6	12.9	84.4
Tinned vegetables	0.0	3.7	40.7	55.6
Tinned fruit	0.0	4.8	42.9	52.4
Dried fruit	0.0	8.7	34.8	56.5
Dried meat	0.0	9.6	28.8	61.5
Tinned/canned meat	0.0	0.0	16.2	83.8

FIGURE 29: Household Food Security Status by Frequency of Purchasing Food Item

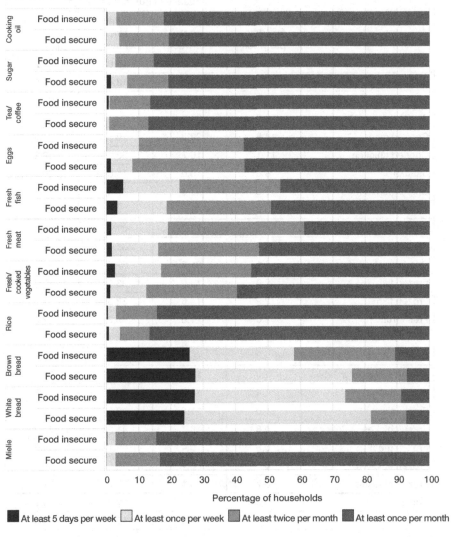

8. HOUSEHOLD AGRICULTURE

8.1 Urban Agriculture

Crush et al. (2011) question whether urban agriculture is a solution to urban food insecurity. AFSUN's work in 2008 found that urban agriculture in Windhoek was almost non-existent with only 3% of households in low-income neighbourhoods involved (Pendleton et al., 2012). More recently, the 2016 survey of the city found that 6% of households were engaged in urban agriculture, which is still a very low figure. In the secondary cities of Oshakati, Ongwediva, and Ondangwa, urban agri-culture is more prevalent with 20% of households growing food. This is a marked drop from an FAO survey in 2000 that claimed that 70% of households in Oshakati were involved in urban agriculture (Dima et al., 2002). However, that was a much smaller sample and their sampling methodology is also unclear.

Of the one in every five households practising urban agriculture in this survey, 95% did so on their own housing plot with a handful (5%) using urban land elsewhere. Maize is not a staple in the area but it is the most popular crop grown (by 45% of households). Other crops grown are veg-etables such as spinach (29%), cabbage (11%), pumpkin (11%), and car-rots (9%). Although growing food in the city is not widespread, Table 25 suggests that households that grow food in the city have a more diverse diet (in terms of the HDDS scores) and a lower HFIAS score.

TABLE 25: Urban Agriculture and Food Security Status			
	Food security scores		
	HFIAS	HDDS	MAHFP
Grows food in town	7.8	5.3	10.8
Does not grow food in town	8.7	4.7	10.8

Why do most households not practise urban agriculture? As many as 80% of households disagreed with the statement that they were not interested in growing food (Figure 30). However, 78% had no access to land, 40% cited lack of skills, and 39% indicated that farming is for the rural poor. Other reasons for not growing were theft (mentioned by 37%), an absence of farm inputs (33%), that it is much easier to buy food (24%), and that they do not have the time or labour (23%).

Around one-fifth of the households in the three towns keep livestock as food, including chickens and guinea fowl (81%), goats (29%), and cat-tle (23%). Pigs, sheep, and donkeys are kept by few households. Urban restrictions on land seems to be a major challenge for households wanting to keep livestock (Figure 31). Many other reasons for not keeping live-stock were similar to those for not growing crops, although significantly more households felt that keeping livestock was a rural activity.

FIGURE 30: Reasons for Not Engaging in Urban Agriculture

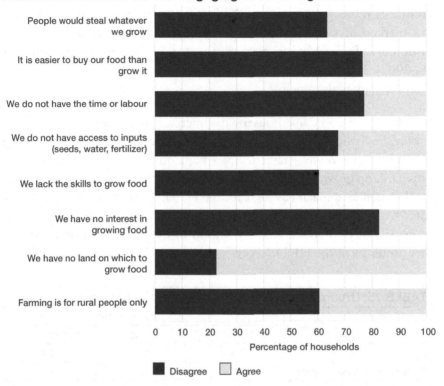

FIGURE 31: Reasons for Not Keeping Livestock in Urban Area

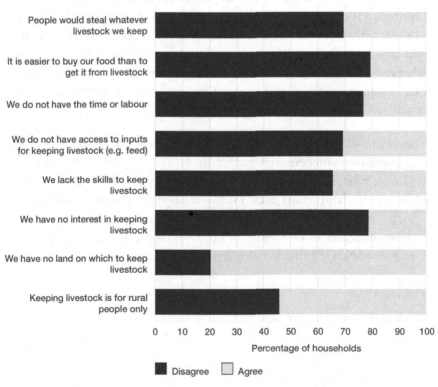

8.2 Rural Agriculture

The proportion of households growing food in the rural areas was much higher (at 42%) than for urban agriculture in the three towns. This is much higher than the Windhoek rate, which helps explain why food insecurity levels are lower in the towns than in the capital. Almost 80% of the households in Oshakati, Ongwediva, and Ondangwa own the land on which they grow crops. The most popular crop grown was the staple food *mahangu* or pearl millet (grown by 41% of all households and 98% of growing households). Other important crops included *omakunde*/cowpeas (82%), maize (67%), *oofukwa*/nuts (66%), sorghum (53%), and pumpkin (47%) (Table 26). Figure 32 shows the percentage of urban households in each income quintile practising agriculture in the rural areas. Interestingly, it is practised most by the poorest and the wealthier households, with over half of the households in the upper quintile engaged in rural agriculture.

TABLE 26: Crops Grown in Rural Areas by Urban Households			
	No.	% of households	% of growing households
Mahangu/pearl millet	351	41.1	98.3
Omakunde (cowpeas)	291	34.1	81.5
Maize	239	28.0	66.9
Oofukwa (nuts)	236	27.7	66.1
Sorghum	223	26.1	62.5
Pumpkin	166	19.5	46.5
Others	37	4.3	10.4

FIGURE 32: Households Growing Food in Rural Areas by Income Quintile

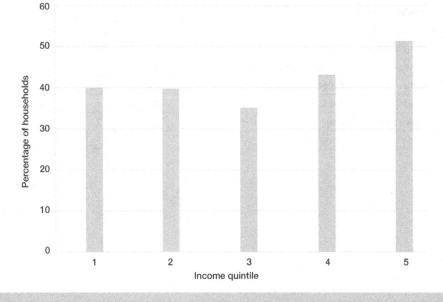

8.3 Rural-Urban Food Transfers

Food transfers from rural households are an important food source and critical livelihood strategy in Windhoek (Frayne, 2001; Nickanor et al., 2016). Frayne (2000) found that 62% of lower-income households in Windhoek receive food transfers from relatives in rural areas, while the 2008 AFSUN baseline survey found that 72% of poor urban households receive food transfers (Pendleton et al., 2012). In the secondary cities of Oshakati, Ongwediva, and Ondangwa, more than half of the households (55%) receive food from relatives in rural areas.

Mahangu flour is easily the most important food item received (by two-thirds of recipient households and 38% of households in total) (Table 27). Over one-third of the receiving households were also sent pearl millet grain. Cowpeas was another important food item received (by 44% of recipients and 25% of all households). Around one-third of recipient households got both fresh and dried wild spinach from the rural areas. As many as 71% of recipients rated them important to the household and 17% said they were critical to household survival (Figure 33).

TABLE 27: Types of Food Transferred to Urban Households			
	No.	% of all house-holds	% of all house-holds receiving food
Uusila womahangu (mahangu flour/pearl millet flour)	325	38.1	68.4
Omakunde (cowpeas)	209	24.5	44.0
Iilya yomahangu (pearl millet grain)	175	20.5	36.8
Omboga (fresh or dried wild spinach)	163	19.1	34.3
Evanda/ekaka/ehanda (dried wild spinach)	151	17.7	31.8
Oofukwa (nuts)	135	15.8	28.4
Eembe (birdplum)	72	8.4	15.2
Uusila wongawa/ongudo (sorghum flour)	53	6.2	11.2
Oodhingu dhonyama (dried beef/game meat)	43	5.0	9.1
Eenyandi (jackal berries)	29	3.4	6.1
Omahuku (marula kernel)	23	2.7	4.8
Note: Multiple-response question			

FIGURE 33: Importance of Food Transfers among Transfer-Receiving Households

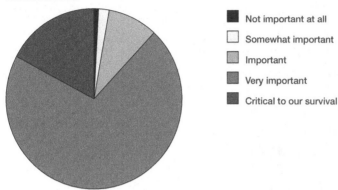

■ Not important at all

□ Somewhat important

▨ Important

■ Very important

■ Critical to our survival

8.4 Indigenous Food Consumption

In Namibia, the term "indigenous foods" is used to capture food that occurs naturally in the environment either as wildlife animal or plant species. Over time, these foods have been integrated into the diet of rural communities. The proximity of communal areas to Oshakati, Ongwediva, and Ondangwa offers important opportunities for the consumption of indigenous foods by urban households. The various indigenous foods consumed by households in the three towns are shown in Figure 34. *Evanda, eembe* and *eeshi* are part of the diet of around 60% of households. *Omagungu* (or mopane worm) is a delicacy consumed in one-third of households, while *oontangu* (kapenta) is consumed by one-quarter of households. In terms of the frequency of consumption, *eeshi, evanda* and *eembe* are all eaten at least once per week by 18%, 15%, and 12% of households respectively. Most of the foods are highly seasonal, however, and tend to be consumed monthly or several times per year rather than year round.

An important question is whether households consume indigenous foods because they cannot afford other foods or because they choose them regardless of their ability to buy food. Figure 35 provides, for each food, the reasons given for its consumption. *Evanda/ekaka,* fish, *omagungu,* and *oontangu* are generally consumed as part of a meal irrespective of whether the households have enough money to buy food or not. *Omafuma* is considered a delicacy and is also consumed regardless. The motivation for consuming indigenous foods is not determined by financial constraints. *Eembe* is eaten as a snack (35%), with other foods consumed as snacks including *eendunga* (12%) and *eenyandi* (9%). Nutrition or health reasons for consuming indigenous foods were cited for *evanda/ekaka* (16%), *eembe* (20%), *eeshi* (15%), *eenyandi* (10%), and *eendunga* (9%).

FIGURE 34: Frequency of Consumption of Indigenous Foods

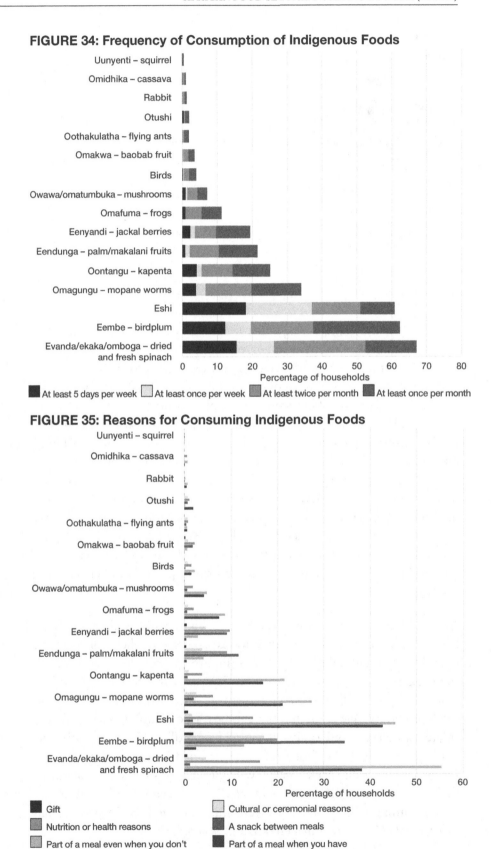

FIGURE 35: Reasons for Consuming Indigenous Foods

Table 28 shows where households obtain their indigenous foods. Some are purchased in markets in the towns (the single most important source) or from street vendors. Others are obtained outside market channels, either sent directly from rural areas or collected by the household in rural areas. Other products are collected by households in urban areas. The relative importance of these different sources varies with the type of food. For instance, *evanda/ekaka* is mostly obtained in markets in the town (42%), sent from the rural areas (38%), or collected in the rural areas (26%). Similarly, *eembe* is obtained in markets in town (43%), sent from rural areas (29%), or collected in rural areas (21%). *Eeshi* is mostly obtained from markets in town (50%), supermarkets (41%), and street sellers (15%). *Omagungu*/mopane worms and *oontangu* are mostly obtained from markets in the towns (64% for mopane worms and 58% for *oontangu*).

TABLE 28: Sources of Indigenous Foods (% of Households)											
	Super-market	Small shops	Mar-ket in town	Mar-ket in coun-tryside	Street seller/ trader	Grown in city by house-hold	Col-lected within urban area by house-hold	Sent from rural area	Grown in rural area by house-hold	Col-lected from rural area by house-hold	Other
Evanda/ekaka/ omboga – (dried/ fresh spinach)	1.2	0.3	42.2	1.2	9.2	1.9	3.1	37.5	4.5	25.5	1.6
Eembe – birdplum	0.2	0.8	43.0	0.6	12.2	2.6	2.8	29.1	3.4	21.2	1.7
Eeshi	40.5	11.2	50.2	2.3	15.3		2.9	9.3		4.8	4.1
Omagungu – mopane worms	0.3		64.0	1.7	18.8		0.7	17.5	0.7	17.8	2.4
Oontangu – kapenta	0.9	0.5	57.7	2.8	23.7		5.1	17.7	0.5	13.0	2.3
Eendunga – palm/makalani fruits	0.5		25.0		2.7	3.3	7.1	36.4	3.8	27.7	4.9
Eenyandi – jackal berries			36.1		4.8	2.4	10.8	35.5	4.8	24.1	1.2
Omafuma – frogs			33.3	2.1	8.3			19.8		28.1	11.5
Owawa/ omatumbuka – mushrooms	1.6		39.3		8.2	1.6	6.6	21.3		24.6	2.6
Birds	2.8		22.2		11.1		8.3	33.3		44.4	
Omakwa – baobab fruit			22.6				3.2	51.6	6.5	38.7	3.2
Oothakulatha – flying ants			29.4		5.9		23.5	17.6		17.6	5.9
Otushi			18.8		6.3	6.3		62.5		31.3	
Rabbit			27.3		9.1	9.1		18.2		45.5	9.1
Omidhika – cassava			44.4					44.4	11.1	22.2	
Uunyenti – squirrel			33.3					33.3		66.7	

9. CONCLUSION

This is the first research report to specifically examine the nature and drivers of food insecurity in the northern Namibian towns of Oshakati, Ongwediva, and Ondangwa. The report argues that the economic, demographic and infrastructural links between these three towns (with their differing origins and functions) justify the label of a single urban corridor. As such, the report focuses on the corridor as a whole, combining the household survey findings from each town into a single data set for analysis. However, it is possible to disaggregate and analyze the results for each town separately if that exercise would be of value to municipal officials and policy-makers in each municipality. The report simultaneously makes a contribution in two other areas of research: first, it is part of a new, and growing, body of research on secondary urbanization and food security in Africa. Second, it makes systematic comparisons between the food security situation in the much larger capital city of Windhoek, where AFSUN-HCP conducted a household survey in 2016.

Rapid secondary urbanization is heavily driven by in-migration from the rural hinterland of urban centres. This phenomenon is certainly true in northern Namibia where over 60% of the household heads in the corridor were born in rural areas (with another 11% born in other towns). Only 22% were born in the three towns themselves. This profile confirms that much of the recent growth of these secondary cities has been driven by in-migration from rural areas. At the same time, half of all household members were born in the three towns, with the proportion born in rural areas only 41%. This suggests that many household heads who migrated to town have remained and their children have been born there. This is confirmed by the age profile of the population, with many residents of working age and many young children.

The obvious question is what kinds of linkages these new urbanites maintain with their rural origins, given both their geographical proximity and, at a broader level, suggestions by some researchers that rural-urban migration in Africa is temporary and circular. This survey did not explicitly set out to examine migrant behaviour but some observations about rural-urban links did emerge. First, high levels of urban-to-rural remittances have been observed in other contexts as a signal of strong backward linkages. However, this survey found that only 27% of households in the corridor remit cash, which is a surprisingly low figure if links are strong (though still higher than from Windhoek at only 18%). Remitting levels do not depend only on rural demand, of course, since the ability of urban residents to remit also depends on their income and other expenses. Since most food has to be purchased, it constitutes a significant expense, along with housing, transportation, public utilities, and fuel. Unemployment levels, particularly in the informal settlements, are high and many households lack the reliable income that comes with regular wage employment. In fact, loss of income and employment were cited as the most significant threats to household food security. Households in the corridor also cannot depend on income from the capital, with just 8% in total receiving cash remittances from elsewhere.

One of the major characteristics of urbanization in Namibia is the perpetuation of rural-urban linkages through informal rural-to-urban food remittances. Previous research in Windhoek has shown that these food transfers from the rural north of the country play a significant role in mitigating food insecurity among poorer households. The question is whether secondary urban centres in the north also experience this phenomenon and, if so, to what extent. The survey found that 55% of households receive food from relatives in rural areas. *Mahangu* (pearl millet) flour is easily the most important food item received (by two-thirds of recipient households). Over one-third were also sent pearl millet grain. Cowpeas and fresh and dried wild spinach were other important food items received.

Another type of rural-urban linkage occurs when urban households farm in nearby rural areas and incorporate that agricultural produce into their diets. Windhoek is a considerable distance from areas of smallholder farming and the prevalence of rural farming by urban households is therefore very limited. In contrast, households in the urban north are potentially better-positioned to farm given the location of the corridor close to areas of significant small farming. The survey found that the majority of households do not engage in rural agriculture, although the proportion that does is significantly higher than in Windhoek. In total, around one-quarter of the households in the urban corridor include their agricultural produce in household food consumption.

An FAO survey of urban agriculture in Windhoek and Oshakati claimed that over 70% of households in both places practised urban agriculture (Dima et al., 2002). This is almost certainly exaggerated since no other studies have reported anything close to these figures. That study even claimed that urban agriculture was more prevalent in Windhoek than Oshakati; another assertion that is contradicted by the 2016 surveys. Less than 10% of Windhoek households are engaged in urban agriculture compared to 20% in the three towns in the north. And while urban agriculture is more common in these secondary urban centres, probably because the climate is better suited and land is more available, it is still the case that most households do not obtain any of their food by growing it themselves.

While Windhoek has undergone a supermarket revolution in recent years, the extent to which South African and local supermarkets have penetrated the country's secondary towns and cities has not yet been clear. This survey showed that over 90% of households in the urban corridor patronize supermarkets, which is a figure far higher than for any other food source. While households tend to shop for staples in bulk at supermarkets, as they do in Windhoek, the survey also found that the proportion of households shopping at supermarkets for particular food items (including fresh produce, frozen produce, processed foods, and cooked foods) was higher than the proportion shopping at every other retail source. While small shops and the open market are important sources for some products, the informal food sector does not appear to be as important in the north as it is in Windhoek. Clearly, distance matters and, although the three northern towns may have fewer supermarkets per capita, supermarkets are probably more accessible to all residents than they are in Windhoek. Therefore, the supermarket revolution may in fact have proceeded further in these secondary towns than it has in the capital.

While the allure of jobs brings many people from poor rural areas to the distant capital, levels of food insecurity in Windhoek are particularly high, especially in the informal settlements that are growing rapidly. Overall, food security is certainly better in Namibia's northern towns with lower mean HFIAS scores, a higher proportion of households in the food secure HFIAP category, and greater HDDS (dietary diversity) scores. However, just because the food insecurity situation is less critical in the north, this does not mean that most households are food secure. Indeed, the majority are not, with more than half classified as severely food insecure by the HFIAP indicator. Like Windhoek, these towns also have considerable income and food security inequality, with households in the informal settlements at greatest risk of chronic food insecurity.

REFERENCES

1. Agada, M. and Igbokwe, E. (2015). "Constraints to Achieving Household Food Security in North Central Nigeria" *Journal of Agriculture and Ecology Research International* 2: 80-86.

2. Botha, C. (2005). "The Odendaal Plan: 'Development' for Colonial Namibia" Department of History, University of Namibia. At: http://www.namibweb.com/oden.htm

3. Carter, M., Dubois, L., Tremblay, M. and Taljaard, M. (2012). "Local Social Environmental Factors are Associated with Household Food Insecurity in Longitudinal Study of Children" *BMC Public Health* 12: 1038.

4. Coates, J. (2013). "Build it Back Better: Deconstructing Food Security for Improved Measurement and Action" *Global Food Security* 2: 188-194.

5. Cockx, L., Colen, L. and De Weerdt, J. (2018). "From Corn to Popcorn? Urbanization and Dietary Change: Evidence from Rural-Urban Migrants in Tanzania" *World Development* 110: 140-159.

6. Cooper, A. (1999). "The Institutionalization of Contract Labour in Namibia" *Journal of Southern African Studies* 25:121-138.

7. Crush, J. and Battersby, J. (Eds.) (2016). *Rapid urbanization, urban food deserts and food security in Africa*. Dordrecht: Springer.

8. Crush, J. and Frayne, B. (2011). "Supermarket Expansion and the Informal Food Economy in Southern African Cities: Implications for Urban Food Security" *Journal of Southern African Studies* 37: 781-807.

9. Crush, J. and McCordic, C. (2017). "The Hungry Cities Food Purchases Matrix: Household Food Sourcing and Food System Interaction" *Urban Forum* 28: 421-433.

10. Crush, J., Hovorka, A. and Tevera, D. (2011). "Food Security in Southern African Cities: The Place of Urban Agriculture" *Progress in Development Studies* 11: 285-305.

11. Dale, R. (2014). *The Namibian War of Independence, 1966-1989* (Jefferson NC: McFarland).

12. Devereux, S. and Naeraa, T. (1996). "Drought and Survival in Rural Namibia" *Journal of Southern African Studies* 22: 421-440.

13. Devereux, S., Fuller, B., Moorsom, R., Solomon, C. and Tapscott C. (1995). "Namibia Poverty Profile" Research Report No. 21, Multidisciplinary Research Centre, University of Namibia, Windhoek.

14. Dieckmann, U. (2007). *Hai//om in the Etosha Region: A History of Colonial Settlement, Ethnicity and Nature Conservation* (Basel: Basler Afrika Bibliographien).

15. Dima, S., Ogunmokun, A. and Nantanga, T. (2002). *The Status of Urban and Peri-Urban Agriculture in Windhoek and Oshakati* (Rome: FAO).

16. Emongor, R. (2008). "The Impact of South African Supermarkets on Agricultural and Industrial Development in the Southern African Development Community" PhD Thesis, University of Pretoria, Pretoria.

17. Frayne, B. (2001). "Survival of the Poorest: Food Security and Migration in Namibia" PhD Thesis, Queen's University, Kingston.

18. Frayne, B. (2004). "Migration and Urban Survival Strategies in Windhoek, Namibia" *Geoforum* 35: 489-505.

19. Frayne, B. and Pendleton, W. (2003). *Mobile Namibia: Migration Trends and Attitudes.* SAMP Migration Policy Series No. 27, Cape Town.

20. Frayne, B., Crush, J., and McCordic, C. (eds.) (2018). *Food and Nutrition Security in Southern African Cities.* London: Routledge.

21. Frayne, B., Pendleton, W. and Pomuti, A. (2001), "Urban Development and Community Participation in Oshakati" In A. Tostensen, I. Tvedten and M. Vaa (eds.), *Associational Life in African Cities: Popular Responses to the Urban Crisis* (Uppsala: Nordic Africa Institute), pp. 282-303.

22. Hangula, L. (1993). "The Oshakati Human Settlement Improvement Project" Discussion Paper 9, Social Sciences Division, University of Namibia, Windhoek.

23. Kakwambi, J. (2012). "Enhancing the Contribution of Small and Medium-Sized Enterprises to Local Economic Development in Oshakati Town, Namibia". MPA Thesis, Stellenbosch University, Stellenbosch, South Africa.

24. Melber, H. (1996). "Urbanization and Internal Migration: Regional Dimensions in Post-Colonial Namibia" Issue No. 48, Namibian Economic Policy Research Unit, Windhoek.

25. Moorsom, R. (1977). "Underdevelopment, Contract Labour and Worker Consciousness in Namibia" *Journal of Southern African Studies* 4: 52-87.

26. Nickanor, N., Kazembe, L., Crush, J. and Wagner, J. (2017). *The Supermarket Revolution and Food Security in Namibia.* Urban Food Security Series No. 26, African Food Security Urban Network (AFSUN), Cape Town.

27. Nickanor, N., Crush, J. and Pendleton, W. (2016). "Migration, Rural-Urban Linkages and Food Insecurity" In J. Crush and J. Battersby (eds.), *Rapid Urbanization, Urban Food Deserts and Food Security in Africa* (New York: Springer), pp. 19-32.

28. Pendleton, W., Nickanor, N. and Pomuti, A. (2012). *The State of Food Insecurity in Windhoek, Namibia.* Urban Food Security Series No. 14, African Food Security Urban Network (AFSUN), Cape Town.

29. Pendleton, W. and Frayne, B. (1998). "Report of the Findings of the Namibian Migration Project" Social Sciences Division Research Report No. 35. Multi-Disciplinary Research Centre, University of Namibia, Windhoek.

30. Tshilunga, S. (2014). "A Study of the 2011 Floods on Human Security in Namibia: A Case Study of the Oshoopala Informal Settlement in Oshakati" MA Thesis, University of Namibia, Windhoek.

31. Tvedten, I. (2004). "'A Town is Just a Town': Poverty and Social Relations of Migration in Namibia" *Canadian Journal of African Studies* 38: 393-423.

32. Tvedten, I. (2011). *"As Long as They Don't Bury Me Here": Social Relations of Poverty in a Namibian Shanty Town* (Basel: Basler Afrika Bibliographien).

33. Weber, B. and Mendelsohn, J. (2017). *Informal Settlements in Namibia: Their Nature and Growth* (Windhoek: Development Workshop Namibia).

34. Werner, W. (1993). "A Brief History of Land Dispossession in Namibia" *Journal of Southern African Studies* 19: 135-146.

35. Werner, W. (2003). "Land Reform in Namibia: Motor or Obstacle of Democratic Development" Paper presented at a Meeting on Land Reform in Southern Africa: Motor of Obstacle of Democratic Development, Berlin.

Printed in the United States
By Bookmasters